Time To Move Forward

By
Patrick Palmer

Copyright 2025 Patrick Palmer
All Rights Reserved

Published by **Native Book Publishing**.

https://nativebookpublishing.com/

Table of Contents

Dedication 1

Acknowledgement 2

Introduction 4

Chapter 1: The Crossroads – Acknowledging the Need to Move Forward 6

Chapter 2: The Seven Stages Of Grief–Understanding And Navigating Emotional Hurdles 11

Chapter 3: Reimagining Life – Crafting a New Vision for the Future 18

Chapter 4: Finding Love Again – Navigating New Relationships 23

Chapter 5: Rebuilding Social Connections – The Power Of Community 28

Chapter 6: A New Home, A New Life – The Symbolism of Physical Spaces 33

Chapter 7: Rediscovering Joy – Hobbies, Travel, And New Experiences 39

Chapter 8: The Healing Power Of Writing – Journaling And Storytelling 46

Chapter 9: The Importance Of Forgiveness – Letting Go Of Guilt And Resentment 59

Chapter 10: Embracing The Future– Final Reflections And Moving Forward With Purpose 67

About the author 77

DEDICATION

To the memory of my loving wife, Angela.

You are in my heart. Forever and always.

Acknowledgement

Thank you, Amy Davis, for your editorial support.

This book is the fourth one in the series. It is the final step in the road to recovery. May you find courage to brave whatever may come.

Introduction

A little over eight years have passed since my beloved wife, Angela, lost her battle with brain cancer. The journey since her passing has been fraught with pain and sorrow, yet there comes a moment when one must look beyond the grief and consider the future. How do I wish to spend the remaining years I have? Should I remain cocooned within the familiar confines of home, or should I venture out to explore the new possibilities that life might hold? I've reached that pivotal crossroads, and it is time to move forward.

According to Emily Long, LPC, "Moving on from grief doesn't mean a static end. It doesn't mean suddenly we're done grieving and will never hurt again. Moving on is more about moving forward than being done."

This book marks my fourth foray into the world of caregiving, grief recovery, and planning for the eventual role of caregiver that some may find themselves in. I am now turning my attention to the question of 'what's next.' This exploration is deeply personal and subjective, as it is for anyone who has endured the loss of a loved one. My intention is to share the aspirations and plans I am now embracing, with the hope that they might resonate with you and inspire your own journey forward.

I am genuinely excited about the future that lies ahead of me. It took me eight years to reach this point. For you, the journey might be shorter or longer, depending on where you are in your own process. But whatever your timeline, it is crucial to start envisioning your future before time slips away.

So, as I set forth on this new chapter of my life, I encourage you to do it with me. Whether you're still navigating the early days of loss or finding yourself at a similar crossroads, know that moving forward is not about leaving the past behind. It's about carrying its lessons and memories with you as you step into the future. Honoring what was while daring to imagine what could be. The road ahead may be uncertain, but it holds the promise of new experiences, growth, and perhaps even joy. Embrace it at your own pace, and when you're ready, take that first step.

The journey is yours to shape.

Chapter 1: The Crossroads – Acknowledging the Need to Move Forward

The Painful Journey

Where do I begin? For eight long years, I grieved Angela, the love of my life. Eight long years of torment, sadness and pain. Those years were some of the hardest times in my entire existence. A truly transformative process that saw me change from what I used to be into the man I am today.

During those eight years, I would have feelings of guilt, sadness, a longing for something that's gone and never coming back.

Nostalgia for the good times, tears for the moments that she was closest to me while I held her in my arms. So many hopes, plans and dreams about the future all shattered. I had gone through a pain that I wouldn't wish on, even the worst of my enemies.

The pain from the loss overwhelmed me like a perpetual dark cloud over my head.

Angela and I had discussed moving forward before her passing. Her words were crystal clear. According to her, six months was the maximum time one should spend grieving, "After that, moving on must be the priority."

I won't lie. Some days were definitely more difficult than others. My family would help me try to get me out of the hole of depression I found myself in, but it was not easy.

It took a lot longer than six months, it seems, but there is light at the end of the tunnel, and I'm here to guide you through it.

Understanding the Need To Move Forward

Let's talk a bit about the very first step that I had to take to move on with my loss. I had to understand and accept that she was gone. No matter how sad I felt, I had to move on and accept the circumstances I was in.

This epiphany came to me after the eight years had passed. I pulled myself by the bootstraps and got to work. The healing process had to begin in earnest.

What It Means To Move Forward

Moving forward is an entirely subjective thing. Everyone has a different view on moving forward. And many people take a lot longer than others when it comes to moving on. That's totally fine. For me, however, I had discussed with my wife what it means to move forward, and she was adamant that the maximum mourning period should be six months, after which moving forward should be the priority. I guess it took a great deal longer than that for me. The very first step I took to move forward came two years after my wife's death.

My brother had convinced me to rent a home in Port Charlotte, Florida. This was far away from the painful memories that haunted me in our vacation home in Maine. The house in Maine where I previously lived embodied Angela's memory, the moments we shared together, and the feelings I was still holding on to.

When I was alone in Maine during the summer months, I was in constant agony due to the memories of Angela. The change in environment was necessary. It allowed me to begin the process of letting go. The house in Port Charlotte eventually became my permanent residence, and I sold the home in Maine to my eldest daughter and her husband.

Eight years is how long it took for me to accept that I needed to move on. For others, it might be different. For me, this was the time it took.

Depending on one's age, employment, health, and personal priorities, there are different timelines for people moving forward.

Over the years, I have noticed many different extremes that people go through when moving forward. Some move to different countries, others marry a new partner within six months, others go back to school to pursue a different discipline, some people travel the world in search of meaning, and some, like myself, do nothing.

The main aspect of moving forward involves opening yourself up to the possibility of loving again.

How to Move Forward

As I mentioned earlier, everyone has their own path in moving on. Some decide to hop on dating apps to find someone, others try to look for the possibility of a relationship through forming new social connections, and others even get married after a couple of months of dating someone new.

There is more than one way to skin a cat. We live in a rather fast-paced world, a world where the ease of technology allows us to meet people far more quickly than we would have otherwise. Social media has its perks.

This does not, however, mean that you absolutely need to move on faster than anyone else. It's your own life and your own journey, which means that you should spend as much time as you need to grieve and mourn the loss of your partner before you decide to move on.

The Grieving Process

There are no set templates or timelines for moving forward. Everyone on this planet has their own unique and personal journey. No one can or should dictate how long it should take for you to grieve. Only we can decide that, and for me, it took me eight years. One thing to remember is the fact that moving forward is not about removing the grief entirely but rather learning to coexist with the grief.

There are different coping mechanisms that people utilize to go through the more intense periods of grief. Some people engage in an intense exercise regimen. Exercise is a powerful way to let out pent-up emotions and is a great coping mechanism. Other people take therapy and counseling sessions to help cope with the pain.

Moving forward is about taking life by the horns. It's about embracing your own truth and accepting that life is unpredictable, which means that it's best to make the most out of the life you have and to honor the life you have lived so far.

Moving forward is also about forgiveness, forgiving yourself for any guilt you might feel, as well as forgiving your partner for leaving you alone on this earth. Forgiveness allows us to lighten the load that we carry, the load being the emotions that leave us depressed, anxious, disoriented and confused. Allowing us to move forward from a place of strength, confidence, hope and a positive attitude.

A Leap Of Faith

Many people, when they are still trying to process the emotions, have many different questions about moving forward. Although everyone might have the same question, the conclusions people draw are often very different.

Is It Possible To Love Again?

This is a good question, and from my own personal experience as well as my observations of other people. I believe that the answer is a resounding 'Yes'. It is indeed possible to move on. Opening yourself up to the possibility of loving someone again is not easy. It comes with plenty of challenges. However, it can be a very fruitful journey.

Does The Pain Ever Go Away?

The pain of loss is a powerful pain that puts many people in a state of melancholy. However, with the passage of time, all wounds heal.

Does Moving On Mean Forgetting?

You will never truly forget someone who played such an important role in your life, but that being said, you will learn to cope better with your situation.

How Does One Cope?

Many coping strategies exist. Some people embark on a physical fitness journey. Exercise and physical fitness are among the best ways for one to improve their physical and mental health. Others go for counseling, and some people turn to religion as believing in a higher power offers solace and peace, especially after a traumatic event such as the loss of a loved one.

Chapter 2: The Seven Stages Of Grief— Understanding And Navigating Emotional Hurdles

Every significant loss in your life comes with its own grief. The grieving process, in terms of its intensity and length, varies from person to person. Some grieve more intensely and for far longer than others. In some cases, people even develop a condition known as prolonged grief disorder.

I spent eight long years grieving. During those eight years, I learned a lot about myself, about what I wanted to do, who I was, and where my life was going. There were many times the grief was unbearable to me.

The Seven Stages Of Grief

The seven stages of grief is a psychological model that was theorized in 1969 by Swiss psychologist Elizabeth Kübler-Ross. She developed it based on the different emotions that people tend to experience after losing a loved one.

Originally, grief only consisted of five stages. In more recent years, it has evolved to about seven stages. Psychological models like this one aren't the be all and end all, and often, you might be going through different emotions that aren't listed in it.

The purpose behind the seven stages of the grief model is to allow yourself to be familiarized with a general guideline that can be helpful during a period of intense grief. Let's take a look at the seven stages.

I'm going to show you how each stage affected me in its own unique way.

Shock and disbelief

This is the very first stage of the grieving process. What separates it from the denial stage is the fact that the individual isn't completely in denial yet but is just unable to even fathom what has happened. The shock is a natural defense mechanism to protect the person from pain. When Angela passed away, I wasn't in shock or even in denial. I simply accepted that it had happened.

Denial

Although this stage is similar to the disbelief stage, what makes denial unique is the fact that it helps one deal with the pain. The way denial works is that the person pushes the thoughts outside of their head or simply acts as if nothing horrible has happened. Some people can get stuck in a long-term state of denial, but this is rare.

Guilt

This is perhaps one of the hardest stages to get through, as it feels like a devastating blow. Questions such as, "What could I have done better?" or "How could I have prevented this?" are very common. Statistics show that around 7% of people go through complicated grief, which is a condition that causes the individual suffering to ruminate over the details surrounding the death. I can say in my case, I was definitely undergoing a great deal of guilt, and it was the hardest part of the grieving process for me. Guilt, in my case, made it difficult for me to find love again, as I was unable to open myself up again.

I had gotten into a relationship with a woman three years ago. She, much like myself, had lost her partner, and although both of us had the same ideas about moving forward, it was quite difficult for me as a result of the guilt. I felt as if I was cheating on my wife due to dating someone new. This was something I had to learn to get through. Guilt had made connecting with someone new very difficult. At the same time, however, I wasn't completely weighed down by guilt because I had done everything I could have possibly done for Angela.

Anger and bargaining

This is the fourth stage and often involves the person lashing out and becoming angry at themselves or the deceased for leaving them behind. I was quite angry at myself and even at Angela for a bit. I was upset that she was gone, and it was difficult to live without the love of my life. So, there would be periods of resentment where I would ask, "Why Angela?"

Depression, loneliness, and reflection

After the acceptance of the loss has happened, the period of depression, loneliness, and reflection begins. This is a time when you reflect back on everything that has happened, the loss of your loved one, the time you spent together with them, as well as acknowledging that things will never quite be the same again. Many people indulge in some rather unpleasant habits during this time. My suggestion is to seek out grief counseling during this time. Being alone with your thoughts during a time like this is dangerous for your long-term mental health and emotional well-being. I remained depressed for quite a long time. In my case, depression would come and go, but with every episode of depression, it would become less and less intense. Among the things that helped me during this time was my family. They would be the ones who pushed me to get out of my head. Talking to them helped a great deal.

Reconstruction, or 'working through'

During this stage, you begin to work on establishing a new 'normal' for yourself. Whatever this might be, you define it yourself. This is the stage where you end up figuring out how to live without them. The loss is still there in your mind; it's still painful, but you have to get through it.

Acceptance

The final stage of the grieving process. This stage comes after you've worked through the pain, the grief, the sadness. This is the stage where you finally realize that your loved one is gone, that nothing can be done, but that you must continue to live and make the most out of your life. Some of the ways you can continue to live during this phase are by getting into new hobbies and socializing with people. During this stage, I recommend going out, socializing, meeting new people, and talking to friends and family. I even recommend traveling to help get through this phase. For me, acceptance came about six months after Angela's death. The very first step after I had accepted her passing was moving from where I lived to a new place.

Why it's important to understand these stages

It's inevitable that you go through them. This will happen, and you will feel miserable, you will feel sad, and you will cry a lot. I know I have. Going through it won't be something that's easy, and it's imperative that you take your time going through these stages. You can't rush through anything. You need to feel the pain. You need to let your emotions out fully. When you experience such a great loss, it's best to shut off all the noise around you, go off social media for a while, and not try to see how other people are living their lives. Try spending time without the internet and without the sensory overload that comes with it.

What is to be done?

The path forward is not an easy one. The journey now involves engaging in new hobbies, rediscovering yourself, separating, and individuating from the past experiences you had with your loved one when you spend so much time with another person, your identity is essentially tied to them, and in relation to them, you need to become your own person again and redefine what it means to be you. You have to rediscover the things that you used to enjoy doing, the things you stopped doing after you got with your partner.

To rediscover yourself, you need to sit in silence and listen to your thoughts, rediscover your authentic voice, and figure out what it is that you like to do; you might have deeply enjoyed a physical hobby before, such as boxing, weightlifting or running and mountain climbing. Try to get back into it, as any form of physical activity is good for you and helps release emotions.

The more you cut out the noise that surrounds you, the noise from past emotions and experiences, the more you find out what your mind and soul need.

Recommendations for dealing with grief

I'm going to give some recommendations as you try to steer yourself through this difficult period. Hopefully, these recommendations will make your journey smoother.

Time Alone Is Important For A While

As discussed during the seven stages of grief, you will have periods where you need to be alone. You should spend time alone and go over your emotions and feelings; you should fully feel what has happened. Let your emotions out and cry even, but after that, you need to start getting out there.

Say "Yes" To Opportunities

Suppose someone invites you to lunch or for a hangout; you might feel the need to stay in isolation, but that is a mistake. Say "yes" to every opportunity that comes your way. Allow yourself to have new experiences; you owe them to yourself.

Open Yourself Up To New Experiences

Life has given you a second chance; it might not be something you wanted, but it's also a gift in its own way. So, don't be closed off. Try to put yourself out there and date new people, see if you're able to connect with someone, and try giving people a chance. You'd be surprised how much this world has to offer you if you open yourself up. Life is meant to be lived and experienced to its fullest.

Seek Therapy

It's important to seek therapy and gain objective advice. We are not in the right headspace when we go through grief. Every thought that we have is clouded by emotions. This makes it difficult for us to see anything rationally. A good professional therapist can help you a great deal to get through this difficult and tumultuous time.

Start Journaling

Writing your thoughts down is a great way to process your emotions, write down how you feel in a journal every single day, and be mindful of what you're feeling when you do. Writing will provide you with a sense of comfort and relief in a time when nothing else will. Writing is also a great way to hold on to the memory of the person you have lost. Writing and journaling were some of the best ways for me to deal with the loss and were even recommended to me by my therapist. Not to mention that journaling was also the reason behind my writing and publishing three books. No specific journal entry stands out, but writing in a journal overall helped me tremendously.

Get Physical

Getting physical refers to engaging in exercise or even a sport. If you have ever enjoyed a sport or a physical hobby, now is the perfect time to get back into it. Exercise has many different advantages. It releases stress, pent-up emotions, and anger. This is among the best ways to cope with what you're feeling during the grieving stage.

These are all the various ways that can get you started on the road to recovery. Grief never quite leaves you; however, you learn to live with it. Appreciate the life you have and make the most of it. Honor the memory of the ones who've passed by living to your fullest.

Chapter 3: Reimagining Life – Crafting a New Vision for the Future

Your New Life

A new life must begin. After passing through the stages of grief, you must begin the journey to move forward and build your life back up again. There are some questions you need to start asking yourself during this period. These questions pertain to what you desire the most from your life and the steps you will have to take. These questions can be as simple as, "What do I enjoy doing by myself?" "What are my goals?" "What is the kind of person I want to be in?" "How can I give value to others?" once you start asking these questions, you will be able to construct a roadmap for the future.

First things first, you have to understand that life is never easy, that there are always going to be roadblocks and hurdles, and you might even find yourself thinking about the past again.

That's totally fine and it's natural to have moments of weakness where you feel as if everything is out of control for you.

Moving forward is all about making decisions to do the things that enrich your life and add value to it. The best possible way you can move forward is by doing new things that make you feel better about yourself.

The Move: Moving On From The Reminders

As I've discussed earlier, the very first thing I ever did was move, and I moved away from my home in Maine to a new home in Port Charlotte. This was a big step that allowed me to finally start again. Now, everyone has a different path to starting their new life. For you, it could be something completely different than for me, but the fact remains that some big changes need to take place.

The home in Maine had become a rather miserable place for me since it was our getaway, a place where Angela and I would create memories. She and I had created memories with our kids as well as our grandkids, and they all had fallen in love with the place. We had a four-bedroom home on a lake. We purchased a kayak, a ski boat, a pontoon boat and a canoe.

I had built a fire pit down by the shore, and it had become a focal point for all of us after the sun had set. I enjoyed teaching my grandkids how to fish. However, once Angela passed, the appeal that the house had for me was also gone. As my neighbors and friends were weekend dwellers, I would feel completely isolated and sad during the week. After her passing, I decided that I was going to be selling the house to my eldest daughter. She was the logical choice since she and her family were very much attached to the property.

Once I had sold the house, I was relieved. Why? Well, the house was staying in the family, and I would not be spending four to five months of every summer completely alone. However, I was also quite sad as a beautiful part of my life had now ended.

Just like the house in Maine was a reminder of all my memories with Angela, you have to move on from the reminders of your own past. How you accomplish this is something that you will have to figure out in your own way.

If you need to change cities to feel better about the situation you're in, you might as well do that for your mental peace because constantly living in the past prevents you from experiencing the present.

Redefining yourself

Give yourself the space to grow and explore new avenues and new hobbies. I believe that physical fitness makes a great starting point, however you don't have to spend hours in the gym to move on from the past. What you need, however, is a good outlet to channel all your negative energy into, and physical fitness provides just that.

There are, however, other things you can do as well, such as painting, arts and crafts, or maybe even playing music or singing. There are many different emotional outlets out there for you to release the feelings of anguish that you might have on your path to healing and building your new future.

Redefining yourself is all about learning and finding new ways to grow as a human being, it's about discovering what it is that you really want from this world and what you can do to make a difference not only for yourself but for others around you. In my case, it was writing books on the topic of caregiving but for you it might be volunteering at a charity or spending some time working at an animal shelter. It could even be something like playing sports with other people. When you're out there focused on something that requires your mental and physical attention, you end up living much more in the present moment, which is a great way to get away from the memories of the past, especially if you do it on a consistent and daily basis.

Anything it is that you feel that you could do that you think could make a difference, do it. This will help you shift the focus from your internal monologue to something in present, to something that might be more productive for you.

New Goals

Sometime after Angela's passing, I worked on writing and publishing books. As a result of working hard on my goals, I managed to publish three books primarily related to being a caregiver. In those books, I expressed what it takes to be a caregiver for someone who is suffering from a serious illness. These writing goals helped me stay focused.

The focus allowed me to create something that I felt was helpful and would provide value to others. The fact is everyone needs goals, and you need these goals to help you move forward in life.

All of us have some major goals we've always wanted to achieve in life. We have to pursue our goals vigorously. Even if we feel down, they become our motivation to keep moving forward, to wake up in the morning, and to have something to look forward to. An important person might not be in our lives anymore, but that doesn't mean that we allow ourselves to stagnate. We have to push through and move forward to achieve the dreams that we've always had.

If you felt that in your whole life, you wanted to learn a specific trade or a skill, then now is the time to start pursuing that. You could sign up for courses and take classes. It can be a great way to meet new people as well.

Another very important thing to remember is that it's not about the destination it's about the journey. It's the little steps that we take to achieve something that makes us feel better about ourselves and makes our days a little brighter. When we see progress, it motivates us to keep going to keep moving forward especially when it feels like all hope is lost.

Social Experiences And Their Importance

Life is a journey that's meant to be shared with others, it's not a journey that's supposed to be experienced alone. You might not have the love of your life with you anymore, but that does not mean that you deny yourself life's greatest gift, that being your fellow humans. You can't isolate yourself from the world simply because it's not good for you.

You require social interaction, just like you require food or water. You must put yourself out there and find other people to bond with.

Putting yourself out there, making new friends, and meeting new people is very important for your mental and physical well-being. We are social creatures, and it's necessary for us to interact with others. It's a need for us, not simply a want. We need to put ourselves out there and build our social circles. It helps to get us out of the rut we often find ourselves in when we dwell on the past too much.

There are many different places you can look at for socializing. Examples include engaging in social hobbies like rock climbing, board games, or simply going for karaoke nights. There are many different things you can do to feel better about yourself. Find something you enjoy doing that you can do with other people and do it. This way, you can make friends with like-minded people with similar interests and hobbies.

Life Is A Gift

Life is a beautiful gift that we all get to have, cherish the time you have on this planet and don't throw it away; things might be difficult, but that does not mean you have to suffer endlessly. You have the capability to do great things and build new and amazing experiences, so allow yourself to experience the beauty of life by going out there and doing new things.

Chapter 4: Finding Love Again — Navigating New Relationships

Love Is A Beautiful Thing

The time is now to finally start getting out into the world and experiencing the love that you have denied yourself for too long. Once you have begun to move forward and passed through the trials and tribulations that come with moving forward, such as the seven stages of grief and spending time alone, you should have a much better idea of the things that you want and don't want. As a result, you are much better equipped to go out and experience love again. This means that you have to get out there and find a partner who understands you and gives you the love that you deserve.

Open Yourself Up

One of the problems that come up often after going through a similar situation to mine is the fact that you find it difficult to truly open up to people due to different reasons, such as the fact that you are somewhat still clinging onto the past and as a result might even feel guilty in a sense for dating someone or trying to find love again. I definitely know I did. You can't allow yourself to feel guilty because it's an emotion that drags you down and keeps you there, not letting you get out there and enjoy the beauty that exists in this world. You have to let go of your feelings of guilt and the whole, "What could have been," mindset that keeps you drawn to the past. To truly move on, you have to embrace the fact that things have changed and that you, as a human being, deserve happiness. Once you truly accept this can, you then begin to open yourself up and find yourself in a situation where you are able to give and receive love.

Happiness

A state of mind that eludes many of us; we find ourselves unhappy due to our circumstances or the events in our lives, which leave an imprint on our psyche, making us sad and depressed. To find happiness, we have to leave the environment that makes us unhappy; for me, it was my home in Maine, and staying there continued to force me to wallow in self-pity and depression. A change in environment and then meeting new people is the key to becoming happy again.

How To Meet New People

Before we can start dating again, we have to meet new people first; we need to socialize and interact with other people. The best way to find someone to date and have a romantic relationship with is through finding people with whom you can engage in shared hobbies. You might be interested in some board games, so go out and play them with others. Who knows, you might just start a conversation with someone, and one thing leads to another, and you end up dating them.

Honesty And Trust

These two aspects are very important. A relationship without good communication, honesty, and trust is one built on a foundation of sand. If you do not trust your partner and don't feel like you can fully open up to them or be honest with them, then you have no chance of making your new relationship work out. It's already difficult when you're going through something as traumatic as losing someone you've loved. To make your new relationship work, you have to be very honest with your partner and have to tell them how you feel about everything in a healthy way.

Openly communicating your desires and your boundaries is key to building trust in a relationship, even if it might be very difficult to do so. Another thing that's often overlooked is compromise. What are you willing to compromise on, and what are you not willing to compromise on? The thing is, we all have our boundaries and are dealbreakers or dealmakers but some things we do have to accept in other people and make peace with and understand. You can't expect to change people if you want to truly give them your love.

Are You Emotionally Ready Or Not?

This is an important question that you need to ask yourself before entering into a new relationship, "Am I emotionally ready to date this new person?" The problem with many people is the fact that they aren't quite ready to start interacting with someone in an emotional and romantic capacity, which leads to them lacking the ability to give the kind of emotional love and support that the other person needs and makes it difficult to sustain a new relationship. There are just so many emotions and feelings that you might have after losing someone. You might be feeling depressed, untrusting, insecure about yourself, and you might not like anything about the world around you even. Another issue that often comes up when we aren't emotionally ready is the fact that we often tend to compare the new relationship to our previous ones, but when we do something like this, we can't allow something new and beautiful to grow and prosper in a healthy way.

Don't Dwell On The Past

Dwelling on the past too much is a common mistake and a common problem that many people have after going through a traumatic event. Long after they've moved on from it, they often still look fondly back on the memories and try to find similarities in people who are just not there. People are much better than you might think.

We become lost in our closed shells, and we don't think too much about the fact that there exists a world filled with people who we just haven't given a chance to. You might have lost your soulmate, but that does not mean there are not beautiful and amazing people out there who can make you feel something amazing that you've never felt before; you can never meet those people if you don't give people a chance.

Long Distance Relationships And Mutual Trust

As discussed earlier, mutual trust is key to having a healthy and sustainable relationship that adds value to you rather than one that puts you in a worse position than the one you were in before the relationship. The relationship that I got into was a long-distance one. When I got into a relationship after Angela's passing, it was with a woman whom I met in my development three years ago. We had a bit of an age gap, and she was also widowed. However, we could only spend 6 months together and then 6 months apart because she was Canadian and was only allowed to be in the US for 6 months. Eventually, however, there was a problem. She called me last September and told me she wanted a full-time romance; this was a horrible blow, and we still remain friends. However, she has moved on with a fellow Canadian.

This relationship taught me a bunch of different things and also gave me purpose after Angela's passing. The fact of the matter is, however, we both weren't quite on the same page, which is why it did not quite work out. In a long-distance relationship, you need to ensure that you and your partner have a mutual understanding on everything.

Embrace Your New Future

The future is bright. There are many beautiful things, places, and people waiting for you. There is so much beauty in this world, and it's meant to be yours. The fact is, if you open your heart, you will get what belongs to you because what's meant for you will always come to you. So embrace your future with open arms and open your heart.

Chapter 5: Rebuilding Social Connections – The Power Of Community

Connecting With People Again

We often find it difficult after a traumatic event to reconnect or form new connections simply because of the fact that the world around us becomes so bleak in our minds. To truly rediscover ourselves, we need to build strong connections with people who understand us and bring us joy. So, how do we go about doing this? The first step I took was moving, and when I moved to Port Charlotte, my brother Tony and his wife Lynn had hosted me a meet-and-greet party. During this party, I met about twenty new people who welcomed me with open arms. Ever since that time, those people have become my close friends, and I often play pickleball and golf with them. We now host dinners after golf on Sunday, on a schedule. These people have become a large part of my life now and have helped me move forward.

Why You Need New Friends

You need to form new memories after losing someone, and it's important for you to find yourself again by meeting new people. The fact of the matter is new people are going to make you feel a lot better about yourself as you will be able to form new memories with them, and this is a big step in moving forward, the formation of new memories, and letting go of old ones. Embracing new people means you embrace a newer version of yourself, letting go of the guilt, the past, and the older things you keep clinging to. Sometimes, we have to find something new to truly grow as people. One of the hardest parts about growing up is the fact that many people tend to drift away from their lives simply due to responsibilities or changing circumstances. After going through a traumatic event such as losing your significant other to an illness, you have to understand that you need to socialize and meet people to grow as a person.

New Avenues For Socializing

Discover different places in your local city to socialize and meet new people. This could be parks, bars, sports clubs, or rock climbing if you're into that sort of thing. The thing is, you need to broaden your horizons, go out, and experience different things that make you feel better about yourself. However, all this being said, you don't have to rush into anything if you aren't fully ready.

Socialize On Your Own Pace

Just like you have to take your time during the grieving process, you also have to take your time during the socializing process, simply because it's different for everyone. Some people are more introverted than others and take more time to open up with people than others. So socialize at your own pace, and don't stress out about trying to make friends if you aren't fully ready to express yourself.

Find Support Groups

Support groups are a great way to socialize and also find people who can sympathize with what you might have gone through, not to mention finding others who could have gone through the same things as you. When we meet people similar to us, we find kinship through similar experiences.

Host Parties or Get Togethers

Once you've made some new friends, you should host get-togethers or parties to get to know people more and form some nice memories with them. This is another great way to socialize and helps you get out of your shell more. A nice get-together party means you get to meet more people.

Focus On Social Hobbies Rather Than Solitary Ones

Get into hobbies that involve socializing and doing something with others. For me, it was golf and pickleball, but the thing is, it can be anything. Solitary hobbies, for obvious reasons, tend to make it harder to socialize, and you end up staying in the same place. Solitary hobbies can be activities such as video games, watching movies, or just reading. It's good to engage with these hobbies on occasion, but if they become the only things you do, you end up finding it harder to meet new people and grow as a person. To grow and move forward, you have to engage with other people and share experiences with them. Oftentimes, it's much harder to express ourselves to people we've just met. However, it's something we have to do if we are to move forward.

Build A Social Circle

The more you socialize and the more friends you gain, the more likely you are to build a strong and productive social circle that can also serve as a strong support network, helping you stay positive and build bonds that will last forever. Humans are meant to be social creatures. You might feel the need to be alone and not talk to anyone for a long time. I did, too. However, we need to socialize to reduce the depression we feel, and even for our own physical health; otherwise, many of the symptoms of sadness, misery, and depression become worse and worse. You cannot wallow in your self-pity anymore. You have to get up and start expanding your network of friends, making new ones, and making yourself feel alive again.

How To Fill The Gaps

After we lose our significant other, we notice one thing: the void that comes as a result of losing someone so important to us. What we end up losing is the social interaction that we used to have with them. For example, with your spouse, they were your source of laughter, your movie partner, they would be your emotional support cushion and make you feel better about yourself. You need to ask yourself if you have friends in your life who fill these gaps, so to speak. Do you know people who can help you fulfill these social needs? And if you don't have these people in your life, then you need to start finding them and meeting them.

Loneliness With A Partner Vs Without

As an introvert, it can be difficult to socialize. However, even introverts need to be with someone to feel less lonely, and this is why even if someone needs solitude in their lives, they can be alone with their partner and not feel 'lonely,' so to speak. When you lose your partner, you don't have this source of comfort anymore, and you can't rely on anyone when you're alone. The feelings of loneliness that come as a result of this can be devastating and harmful. One of the reasons that makes losing your partner so much more devastating is the fact that now you can't talk to anyone after a rough day at work or after feeling overwhelmed, with no one to reassure you. This is why you need to grow your social circle to have people you can quietly sit down with and talk to when you feel lonely. Another thing that comes as a result of this is the fact that you can also potentially find people that you might want to become romantically involved with. As discussed in the previous chapter, you have to learn to move forward and find love again.

Strength In Numbers

A lone wolf can't survive in this world. There is a great deal of strength in numbers. The more people you meet and the more people you connect with, the greater your energy and positivity. The more you learn, the more you grow as a person. The fact is you have to put yourself out there to gain back the energy that you once had. Move forward with strength and find people who reflect the positive energy you give to them.

Chapter 6: A New Home, A New Life – The Symbolism of Physical Spaces

Our Ability To Attribute Things

We have this powerful capability as humans to attribute things or give meaning to things or places. It's a topic discussed quite a lot in psychology. Attribution theory is a theory that tries to explain how we perceive causes of events and behaviors. It primarily has to do with how we attribute success and failures to both ourselves and others.

We attribute many things to the place where we live, and if you shared a home with your significant other and they are no longer there with you, then well, you will attribute all the memories of the past and the lost future to that place.

Why Do We Have To Move

The lost need to be left behind; the ones who have passed need to leave your mind. Mementos of the past are things that need not be with you anymore. The choice to leave behind everything and start again is a choice that I had to make for myself when it came to my move.

The decision to move to Port Charlotte, leaving behind my home in Maine, was a decision that was not easy to make, but it was necessary because of the weight that was holding me back there. The past needs to go; the past is painful, and it hurts.

Your brain simply serves as an organ that hurts you with the memories of the past. As a result of this and other unpleasant feelings you are having in association with the past, you need to make a large change in your life. You need to start cutting things off.

This is very similar to cutting a piece of your own body off; you shared every moment with this person, and now you have to cut off the things that were there with you at one point. This is not easy or painless; it's a process that hurts immensely, but it needs to be done.

This process requires losing so much, but in the end, it will all be worth it. You, as an individual, need to heal because you're not doing a favor to anyone when you hold on to the past.

A New Life Requires Change

To truly move forward and become a different person, you have to want it badly enough and make changes that are very painful and uncomfortable for you in the present moment.

The thing is, it's easy to be cynical and jaded. Staying in one place and feeling bad about yourself is the easiest thing in the world; it requires no effort to do so.

To actually change and move forward, you have to go through something painful and difficult and accept that it's not going to be easy. A new place, a new home, and a new city. These were the changes I took, and all of them contributed to my healing.

Symbolism Of Physical Spaces

There is a great deal of symbolism behind physical spaces; the places where we live and spend our time, especially when it's with someone else, mean a lot to us.

The idea of a place being symbolic is the meaning it gives to you, and if you find that the only meaning you get from the place is holding on to old memories of someone you cared for immensely, then that place no longer exists to serve you but rather work against you.

If you're still living in a place where you built and created memories with someone, those same happy memories are now going to be the very source of your emotional anguish. Anything that can build you up has the power to destroy you completely.

For this reason, you cannot stay in the same place anymore. You have to move forward, you have to leave it behind, and you have to make the change to go someplace else.

The world is a large and beautiful place that's meant to be explored. If need be, you might even change your country if that's what it takes for you to move forward, but it's not so bad in the grand scheme of things if you want to find mental peace.

A place only matters to us as much as the value we give to it. The fact of the matter is there is a great deal of peace that can be found anywhere in the world.

I built a whole life with Angela in that place and made amazing memories there. Staying there was just not in the cards for me. I couldn't do that. There were so many plans that we had that were all gone. They were all lost, so staying there was just a constant reminder of all that could have been.

You don't need to stay in one place if it brings you pain. You're not on this earth to suffer. You're here to thrive. You can't thrive with too much mental pain. It destroys the brain bit by bit. You're here to live, not to let the pain eat you up.

The Symbolism Of The New Home

The new home in Port Charlotte represented symbolically a new time in my life, a new version of me. It showed that I was, at the very least, trying to finally move forward. That I was becoming myself again and finding myself again.

After moving to Port Charlotte and making new friends, I did start to feel a little bit better about myself. After moving, I also got into a relationship with someone, and even if it didn't work out, I still learned a lot. It's never too late to grow again, to start learning again, to start living again. You'll never be too old for those things. If you are alive and breathing, then there are still so many things to live for that you are missing out on when you hold onto the memories of the past.

The Beauty In Letting Go

Letting go of places, people, and periods of time. These are necessary steps to take to move forward with your life. They have to be taken if you want to grow as a person. If you want to continue in self-pity, then what you might be doing right now is perhaps fine.

However, no one wants to live like that for an extended period of time. It's not healthy. We all have our goals and ambitions in life. If you had goals in life back then that pertained to you and you alone, now is the time to focus on them and achieve them. Holding on and staying in one spot simply means that you're allowing your own self to pass away with the past.

Misery Is A Disease, Moving Forward Is The Cure

The cure to holding on, the cure to stagnation and being miserable, is simple. It involves you leaving behind the things that hurt you, the things that make you feel bad, and it's a disease with only one treatment: moving forward.

The fact of the matter is you have to remove the pain that keeps you trapped in one place for so long. The pain never truly goes away, the things that hurt you, that make you feel bad. To remove those things from your life, you have to organize things, the things that you want to keep and the things that you want to remove.

What Is The Significance?

Symbolically speaking, moving to a different place entirely in a different city for me was a symbolic representation of letting go. It was very significant for me to cut out her memory, the memories that I built and shared with her, and although the home in Maine stayed in the family, I was no longer in that home. I was removed from that place and that situation where I felt as if I was just wallowing in self-pity.

I had a reason to leave it. The reason was plain and simple. Maine held nothing for me anymore in terms of fulfillment and happy life; in fact, it was antithetical to those very things. It brought back feelings of negativity that needed to be cut out.

Why Is It So Hard?

Every single thing worth doing in life is hard. This is something that applies to becoming successful as well, but it is very true when you need to regain your sense of self and happiness. Separating and individuating, becoming your own person again, and finding new people to talk to and socialize with are things that every person needs to do after such a long gap of not interacting with anyone.

I knew for myself that if I had never let go, I would have stayed depressed and that if I hadn't moved away from that home, I would have felt sad, depressed, and unsure of myself. I knew I had to do it because it was the only way out of a difficult situation.

As a result, I made the effort to do it. You will have to make decisions similar to what I had to do in my place; it might not be the exact same, but it will be similar.

A place, object, or home is only as important to us as our relationship to it. If that relationship is tainted with bad memories, then we have to get rid of it. It's the equivalent of holding onto an arm that's been infected, and the infection grows until you are consumed by it.

As harsh as these words may sound, the unfortunate truth of the matter is that when you stay in one place that makes you dwell on the past for too long, then it is going to be damaging for you and your well-being. The decision to walk away is something you need to do.

Walking Forward Toward Happiness

The bleakness is over. The move has been completed. You are free now to move forward and embrace a new existence in your new city, home, country, etc. The fact of the matter is you are not the same as you used to be, and that's a good thing; the scars will fade even if they don't fully heal.

The world awaits you. Work towards your goals and become whole again, becoming a beacon of light for the people around you because although we truly live, only once do we have the power to make a good impact on the world and make it somewhat better.

Even if we feel that our actions are minuscule in the broader scope of the universe, we are still capable of doing good and pushing the world in a positive direction.

Chapter 7: Rediscovering Joy – Hobbies, Travel, And New Experiences

Find Your Own Way To Happiness

We're born not to suffer. We're born to live. Suffering is inevitable, but living a happy life is something we choose to do. Our pursuit of happiness involves finding ways to make the time on this rock more meaningful and more enjoyable. So, how does one go about accomplishing this level of happiness and contentment? Well, the first thing you have to do is let go of the metaphorical chains that bind you and hold you back. Through careful deliberation and a strong focus, you have to motivate yourself to go out there with the goal of finding something interesting to do. The way we accomplish this is by finding the right hobbies and interests that we can engage in, ones that make us connected to other people.

These hobbies can include but are not limited to playing a sport or joining a book club. You could even join a chess club if it provides you with opportunities to socialize. You have to put yourself out there and meet people who will eventually make a difference in your life. These hobbies can also be something you used to do but stopped doing altogether when you got with your partner due to a possible lack of time. The beauty of engaging in hobbies that mean something to you is the fact that they bring you a sense of joy and, in the case of sports, can even instill a sense of discipline within you.

If you have no hobbies, that's okay too; now is the time to discover something new, something that makes you feel better about yourself. This is the time to find out what it is that makes you feel better. What do you enjoy? Maybe some soul-searching is required to truly figure this out. But the best advice in a situation such as this is to go out there and do anything. When you do something, even if you aren't the best at it, you will find that it will bring you joy and happiness.

Travel Is A Powerful Experience

Now, let's look at some other things that you can involve yourself in that can make you feel a lot better about yourself. If you want to travel, The joy of travel is the fact that it lets you see new places, explore different avenues, and discover yourself. Travel is really special because it makes you feel alive, when you see a completely different culture compared to yours, you find yourself feeling very different about yourself and how you perceive the world, seeing people go about living their lives in a foreign land is going to make you feel something different and new, this is exactly what you need to experience right now. Something different and new from the constant routine of feeling bad on a daily basis. Take the plunge and go out there. You'll be pleasantly surprised when you see how unique and different so many places in the world are.

When you travel, in a sense, you choose to let go of the memories. You choose to explore something new, and that on its own is an empowering experience. You make the decision to be somewhere else in the world where the past does not haunt you, and as a result, you become freer. It's quite liberating, really. You are free to do anything. Now, I understand it might not be the easiest option to get up and travel, but nothing worthwhile ever came easily.

The fact is traveling will make you understand more about yourself and the world than you could ever hope to imagine. When you travel, and especially if you go around the world, even to places that might not be as financially stable as the United States, what you will find will truly show you that we only really have one life to live and that we're very privileged to have the things that we do have. It can always be so much worse. This really sets things into perspective and gives you a greater motivation to live your life to its fullest. It also allows all the happy moments to shine bright while letting the sad moments fade away.

Appreciate The Time You Have

You do have to understand something very important: this gift of life that we have is temporary, and it's far more limited than we think. We can't just let it pass us by because we can't afford to. The time we spend reminiscing on the past is time we can use to do something new and better because we can spend the remainder of our lives being miserable and depressed, and we all know how that ends: many turn to drugs, alcohol, or other forms of escape to numb the pain. It's a sad reality that many just can't handle what life throws at them and resort to walking on the wrong path to cope. The limited time that we have should be spent doing the things that bring us joy and peace, not things that cause us to wallow in our own self-pity.

What Travelling Did For Me

When I traveled, I went from Maine to Port Charlotte, and when I got to Port Charlotte, I started dreaming about the future. How it happened was that my brother had suggested that I come to Florida to get away from the grief within my house.

I rented for three months, then three months the second, and then I bought a house in Florida in a residential home development for 1800 people. I sold my house in Maine to my eldest daughter and her husband because the home in Maine was too quiet for me, forcing me to wallow in my own self-pity.

In Florida, there are an endless amount of activities and clubs that I can engage with, making it impossible for me to be alone for any significant period of time, which is really perfect because it allows me to discover happiness again. I have been into athletics my whole life, and the community I live in offers me all the sports/facilities that I've always enjoyed. These include golf, tennis, and pickleball, and engaging in these hobbies has made me realize what happiness truly is.

Happiness is all about being there in the present moment and appreciating this gift of life, knowing that just the fact that we're still alive and breathing is a miracle on its own.

When we are happy, the fears of the future and nostalgia for the past don't bind. This is why, logically speaking, our purpose needs to be to seek out that which brings us pleasure and gives our life meaning, whereas we reject that which harms us and minimizes the kind of life we can enjoy.

The enjoyment that we can gain from life is immeasurable if we just let ourselves have it. A part of me is still Angela, and I still become sad when I remember her and look back at everything. But to embrace the new chapter of my life, I can't deny myself joy and happiness.

It's not something I can afford to do because life is a gift, and we can't squander this gift. We just can't do that. We have to make the most of it.

Rediscovering Joy, Embracing Happiness, Letting Go

To rediscover joy and embrace happiness, you have to let go of the weight of living in a place that makes you feel the loss. Everything is temporary. Nothing lasts forever, and living in the present moment is the best we can do. Everyone makes memories.

Those memories are really pleasant when we think about them. Just be happy you were lucky enough to experience something that not everyone gets to have. Not everyone is lucky enough to have someone that they loved and, cherished and felt loved in return. Not everyone is lucky enough to have that. But those memories and those feelings of clinging on to the past are not good for the soul, not anymore.

Gain New Knowledge

You choose that which benefits you, and as such, you must fill your mind with something that helps you grow as a person rather than something that only seeks to harm you. Read books when you are alone and you feel sad; read something that teaches you something new, something you never really knew before. Invigorate your mind by reading something that truly requires you to think.

This could be philosophy. Philosophy is a great discipline and tries to help us live in accordance with the nature of the universe. It opens our eyes to understanding reality better. Gaining knowledge is good for the mind. It allows the mind to recover and allows you to have a more balanced perspective on everything because your mind is filled with something productive rather than sad memories of the past.

This can also be applied to other things as well. You could maybe pursue a small course or a degree in something that you always found fascinating. Studying helps us focus and discipline ourselves because when we work on learning new things, the mind is strengthened. The mind is utilized to a higher degree, and thus, you gain something useful out of it. It won't completely cure the pain. Nothing except time can help you with the pain, but it can offer a healthy distraction that puts your brain in a focused state.

The focus that you gain from studying can be applied to other things in your life as well. You can use the newfound focus to work to make your business better or start a new business of your own. You can focus on doing many things that can bring you happiness. Consistency, focus, and thinking outside the box can take you places you never thought were possible. Just pour the pain that you feel into something, and you will see that the results you gain from just showing up and doing something will be worth the efforts you make.

The efforts that we make in life have an impact on our well-being, and they provide us with a sense of direction. All the effort that we put into something when we put our heart and soul into something.

Eventually, we achieve something that makes us proud to be alive. The sense of accomplishment that comes from winning is unparalleled. If you allow your life to stagnate without anything to show for it, every pain that you've ever felt will only get worse. So, you have to move forward and progress in life.

Your Progress Through Life

An object in motion stays in motion unless acted upon by an external force. An object at rest stays at rest unless acted upon by an external force. This is Newton's first law of motion. It applies to you as well.

Progress in whatever it is you seek to do in your life can only happen when you get up and do it. If you have some ambition that requires you to work hard to get good at it, then you must do it with vigor.

It's never easy to start; the first step is the hardest, but you have to start, and when you do start, the progress that you gain from working towards your goals will motivate you to push forward it will motivate you to get even better. This forward momentum is only going to help you move forward at a rapid pace. You'll reach a point where you find that you're far happier than you ever dreamed of. Trust the process, too.

Sometimes, when we feel like nothing is working even though we're trying so hard, it's only because we aren't looking at the bigger picture. Incremental baby steps take us a lot further than we could ever imagine.

Get Your Life Back

It's time to take control of things that you felt were out of reach, go out there, and start doing the right things that bring you joy and not sadness or negativity. Work hard, stay consistent, and find your own way to happiness. Don't dwell on the past. The time to move forward is now.

Chapter 8: The Healing Power Of Writing — Journaling And Storytelling

The Mindset That You Need To Have

What makes journaling and writing, in general, such an oft-given piece of advice when dealing with something heartbreaking and traumatic? Well, the answers to that are quite simple: journaling your thoughts in a positive and healthy fashion allows you to express your emotions and feelings in a way that not only clears your own mind but also brings a sense of peace to your soul.

The reason is simple: when you objectively analyze a situation and write it down, the positive thoughts, neutral, and negative thoughts that you have when they are written down provide a sense of clarity to your own mind. Not at first, it takes its time, but it plays a large role in your road to recovery over time.

However, there are ways to go about this. Some ways are more correct than others. If you simply use journaling as a form of venting without any productive end, then this can be very counterproductive in the long run. You have to come up with a solution to move forward and to gain a better idea of how forward momentum in your life is still possible.

Journaling allows many people to discover what's deep inside of them and the type of lives that they want for themselves because when you start writing your thoughts down, you detect certain patterns of thinking that can be useful for you in learning more about yourself.

These patterns of thinking allow you to fully figure yourself out. Well, we don't always fully figure ourselves out because that's long-term and ongoing progress; however, we understand the things that make us feel whole.

The idea of wholeness is doing something that provides us with a sense of accomplishment, meaning, and a deeper understanding of who we are as individuals and what our desires might be.

Another benefit of journaling is the fact that it's simply on a piece of paper. No one has to look at it. No one has to know what you're thinking about because it's all on a piece of paper or a notebook that only you have access to and no one else.

Identification Of Patterns

Everyone functions and goes through life on the basis of certain repeating patterns. They are compelled to behave or act a certain way because of the experiences that they've had in life, good, bad, or both, but usually, trauma is something that tends to cause people to act in a certain way, which is why we have to pay closer attention to the effects that trauma can have on our psyche.

Become Honest With Your Self

Most people are unfortunately not very honest with themselves about a great deal of things, specifically, the circumstances they find themselves in, the causes of events, or the reasons for themselves being the way they are.

What many people think they know is simply a biased perspective that they have developed about themselves. We don't even fully understand why we behave or react to things the way we do. The reason is that we lack awareness. We aren't fully in control of many of the functions that we engage in. This is where journaling truly shines. It allows us to expose ourselves to us.

For journaling to be effective, it has to be done with a strong and deliberate effort, and one must be honest with oneself. Without honesty, you are left with a journal that only tells half of the story or a quarter of the story, which is very unproductive and does not lead to the benefits that journaling can provide.

Don't Just Throw Your Emotions Be Productive

Sometimes, we do need to just vent our emotions in a journal or a piece of paper. Sometimes, it's important that we do. However, it's not something we can keep on doing forever because it keeps us wallowing in self-pity and staying stuck in a depressive state instead of gaining the forward momentum needed to move through life and become productive and happy.

In this case, for example, you are writing about everything that has happened that's made you sad or uncomfortable. Write down your feelings on why, then think of a healthy solution or a coping mechanism and write that down. The way we go about doing this matters a great deal if we wish to become better individuals, be mentally healthier, and be able to move forward from any tragic circumstances that might have fallen on us.

Reading Your Entries

When you read your entries, especially your older ones, it helps because you get to see the emotional progress that you've made. It lets you let go of the past memories and the pain that you were holding on to over time.

The fact of the matter is that many of the memories you hold onto that torment you or make you feel unhappy with yourself are memories that you have been unable to cope with due to resistance. Journaling allows you to break your defenses and find new solutions to move forward, which will help you cope far better.

This also leads you to make new goals that can benefit you and to have a purpose in life again, a real purpose that brings you deeper satisfaction and meaning.

Start Writing About What Makes You Happy

It could be a nice song, a wonderful movie, or a book you read. It could even be a sport that you enjoy engaging in. When you write about the things you enjoy, write and describe why you enjoy them. What are the aspects of those activities that make you feel alive? What are the ways in which you can enjoy those activities more?

You have to look into the finer details about what you like to do in your spare time, whatever it is that makes you feel better about yourself, because this allows you to understand the positives and thus maximize them.

Most people don't truly know why something brings positive emotions within them, so it's good to have a clearer picture of that. When you truly understand yourself, then figuring out what the right thing to do is no longer hard.

Start Writing About Your Goals And Ambitions

Goals and ambitions are things that everyone has, just like everyone has opinions. There is something deep down that you know you want to do, but the fear of failure and uncertainty prevent you from trying.

So start writing about it. Write about your fears and uncertainties, but also write about the methods that you will take to overcome them. Even if it's just one positive thing that you can think of writing, do it. It will help your mind get out of the rut it's in. So start working on your goals. We all have our dreams, and it's up to us to make them a reality.

Focus On Improvement Rather Than Staying in One Place

Focusing on moving forward should be the goal. This applies to everything that we do in this book, and journaling is no different. Make sure that whatever you write, you write with the objective of moving forward, not staying stuck in the memories of the past. The past is the past; it's gone now, and for better or worse, we don't really have the ability to change anything or to go back in time and make a difference.

You need to be writing with the intent to move forward. The journal entries, more than anything, need to show a genuine effort to move forward. Forward momentum is what's going to keep you going, not stagnation.

The essence of moving forward is all about staying in motion. You don't stay in motion when all you do is keep looking back at nostalgiac feelings of the past and the way someone you cherished deeply made you feel.

Because as great as anyone is, everyone's time on this earth is temporary, including yours. So just make that effort to let go of the chains that bind you to a past that brings you nothing but sadness.

It's not productive to continue to feel this way after a certain point has passed. You have to understand that sometimes, we need to pull ourselves out of a hole that we have dug ourselves into.

Why do we do this to ourselves? Even if we logically understand that's not the best thing to do, emotions are never rational. Emotions are not something you can stop or, shut down or control.

Nothing about us exists in a vacuum. Even the most hardened stoic feels intense emotional pain when something bad happens to them because, at the end of the day, we are humans and not emotionless robots designed to do things. There is far more to us as a whole than just doing things.

Our mind is a complex place where so many different functions are happening all at once. We have to be aware of the fact that whatever we're feeling right now is a result of circumstances beyond our control.

Look At What You Can Control

You can't do much for someone who's no longer with you. The most you can do is honor their memory. But what is it that you can control? What are the aspects of your life that need correction? When you work on those aspects, you will come to a better understanding of yourself.

You could be overweight. For example, embarking on an exercise and diet regime can give you a sense of purpose and direction. You could be someone who isn't satisfied with the career that they have chosen for themselves; now is the time to enroll back in school and gain the knowledge needed to better yourself.

You have to control what you can change, and what you can't change needs to not take up mental space in your head. Your mind is a powerful tool and a very precious thing that you can't afford to waste.

Your brain should be filled with positive ideas for the future. Grow your mind, engage in activities that grow your mind.

Do not engage in memories that keep it stuck in one place. The mind can be damaged by many different things that hold it back. This could be clinging on to damaging beliefs, bad memories, or even the influence of bad people.

Journaling Provides A Sense Of Clarity

Journaling is the gift that allows you to see everything for what it is. You get to see the flaws in your own thinking, you get to observe everything around you, and you find out what is wrong with you. The beauty of journaling is the fact that you can observe the problems, the positives, and everything there is in an objective sense. This level of objectivity allows you to cut out the clutter, so to speak. You are able to remove the things that do not benefit you in any way and rationally move on with the things that do aid you.

We Are All Travellers On A Journey

Your journey needs to be defined by the successes that you have and not your failures. Failure is a part of life, but it's not who you are. Everyone holds immense potential that only truly comes out when they allow it to. The potential that's untapped and held deep within. This is something that you need to unleash for yourself rather than drag yourself into a pit of darkness from which there is no recourse.

Journaling Provides Long-Term Benefits Not Short-Term

Let's take, for example, two people. One of them journals for a couple of days to let go of his traumatic past and solve his emotional problems. Unfortunately for this guy, he has no direction, does not even know what to write meaningfully, and expects journaling to solve all his problems in a single day. The second guy does the opposite. He journals for months.

This process of journaling involves him asking meaningful questions about himself and the things that might have happened in his past that have held him back. His approach to journaling is productive as it works on the basis of solving problems rather than simply venting.

The latter person is the approach you need to be taking; journaling is something you are in for the long haul, not for instant gratification, which seems to be so popular these days.

Journaling won't instantly fix your problems and help you cope with everything. No, it will simply serve as a way for you to find your own solutions and help you heal and grow day by day, bit by bit.

Imagine this: there's a man out there who wants to somehow look like the guy on the cover of Men's Health. He tries to work out but gives up after a month because he looks nothing like that. However, another person sticks with it, works out consistently for years, and eventually even surpasses his own idol.

What made the second person successful and the first person not? The second person was successful because he understood that everything in life that's worth having comes from consistency, delayed gratification, hard work, and a disciplined approach. You gain absolutely zero when you have no consistency or discipline in life. Everything requires discipline, patience, and the drive to see things too till the very end.

You have to do the right things whether you feel like doing them or not. You have to get up in the morning and journal. You have to go out, socialize, and make friends and connections because even if it's difficult, it's something that is important for you and your mind; you also have to take up therapy because a professional is far more objective about things than you can be. The hardest tasks or activities in life are the ones that bring the most growth in us as humans.

Healing Does Not Come Without Effort

The one thing that everyone seems to forget about the healing process is that you need to embrace pain. You need to embrace the pain. You have to walk towards the things that you fear the most because if you run away from them, then you end up in a situation where they overwhelm you because you can't hide from things forever. You have to face them. You can't numb your emotions and pretend that everything is fine. You have to embrace the very thing that hurts you because it's a part of you that you can't just ignore. Learning to live with it is what you need to start doing.

The funny thing is that quite a great deal of people are under the false presumption that they can simply heal without having to do the hard work of embracing adversity and difficulty. You can't do that. Look at it this way.

A medicine that is bitter tends to produce the result of healing. When you have a physical wound that is large, and you try to heal it, it hurts, it's not comfortable, it's not painless, and it's not easy. There are no easy solutions to any real problem.

Every difficult problem has a solution that involves some sort of challenge, some sort of difficulty. The only reason we are stuck in the same spot is because we are ignoring reality and choosing to run from a problem that's there.

Journaling Is One Tool, Not The Solution

There is no single solution for moving forward because moving forward comes from the interplay between the various different actions that you take. Much of these have been discussed earlier in the book. Journaling is simply a tool. It can be a very effective tool over time, but it's just that, a tool.

Do not consider it to be everything in your journey to healing. You still need to make decisions for yourself that benefit you, such as moving from where you live to a different city/country, socializing and meeting new people, dating again, etc. Journaling is just one thing that helps you ground yourself.

Some Tips For Journaling

To make your time journaling the most effective and productive as it possibly can be, I'd like to provide some tips that can prove to be helpful:

1. Set A Regular And Consistent Schedule For Journaling: As I previously discussed and stressed the importance of consistency, you need to be journaling on a consistent basis, ideally at a specific time every day or every week. The frequency depends upon you.

2. Make Sure Your Space Is Comfortable: The best place for journaling is one without any clutter or noise so that your thoughts are free to leave your mind and gently touch the pages of your journal.

3. Honesty Is Key: The idea behind journaling is to be as honest as possible. Do not judge yourself for writing something that you might find to be outlandish or strange. No one is judging you. You have the freedom to write whatever you want, so be as authentic as you can be.

4. Combine Journaling With Therapy: The idea is to combine your journaling with other sources of emotional support, such as Cognitive Behavioral Therapy (CBT), and also discuss your journal entries on a consistent basis with your therapist.

5. Look Up Journal Prompts: These can provide ideas or inspiration to make your journaling far more productive and helpful. Some good examples of prompts can include:

What is holding me back?

What do I need to let go of?

What is the weight that I am carrying?

What shame do I live with?

What is preventing me from moving forward?

6. Journaling Initially Causes Pain: This is just something you need to keep in mind. When you first start this process, it will be painful, but this pain will subside and will be replaced with strength and confidence.

Writing And Storytelling: How It Helped Me

Storytelling is A Powerful tool

I've discussed so far how we need to find a way to get back into the groove of things, forward momentum, so to speak. Everyone has their own approach to this sort of thing, but writing is the one that helped me the most. Writing books on being a caregiver allowed me to provide value to people and share many of the experiences that I had as a caregiver for my wife, Angela, who passed away.

Writing allowed me to take the immense pain I had and translate it into something that can guide people and help them during a very difficult period. I can tell you for a fact that being a caregiver is a lot of work, emotionally, mentally, and physically. Many who are in the position that I was in have no real guide or method to truly help them out. So, I wrote my book to help those people as well as provide a sort of catharsis for myself.

Writing Is Art, And Art Is Self Expression

Self-expression gives us the ability to show how we feel to the world. It allows us to release that which we hold internally out into the world. No longer are we keeping it all inside of us; we are letting those emotions run free, and we are allowing them to be let loose.

Journaling and the books that I wrote went hand in hand because journaling was the basis for my books. Much of what I was going through became a part of the books that I wrote, and it paved the way for me to move forward and let go of a past that haunted me.

The books that I have written so far have continued to motivate me to keep writing, as I feel that for me personally, writing and journaling are both very cathartic. Writing has given my life purpose and direction. It can serve as something similar for you, but I recognize the fact that everyone is different and has their own purpose.

It Never Gets Easier You Just Become Stronger

The road to healing never becomes any less harsh. It doesn't become any easier. However, after learning the lessons, adopting healthy coping mechanisms, and making conscious and motivated efforts to move forward, we are able to persevere.

Chapter 9: The Importance Of Forgiveness – Letting Go Of Guilt And Resentment

Forgiveness is non-negotiable. You have to forgive the person that's no longer with you. And even if you don't want to, you also have to forgive yourself.

At the end of the day, holding onto the past, the memories of the past, and the negativity that it brings are things that are going to stall your growth. Forgiveness is perhaps the final stage of letting go because of the simple fact that when you forgive both yourself and the ones who are gone, you are at peace. When you are finally at peace, you can embrace yourself.

We hold onto so many different things that bother us, and we continue to hold onto them, forgetting ourselves in the process. We can't keep doing that to ourselves. Only when we learn to forgive both ourselves and the other person can we learn to move forward and grow as human beings.

The focus of forgiveness is about bringing back the energy that you expended on someone else onto yourself. You bring it back to yourself so you can have a better sense of control and are able to act in a manner that is far more productive and healthy for yourself and for the ones closest to you who are still with you.

Energy And It's Use

There's a finite amount of energy within all of us. We have a few choices: We can utilize them in the things that can provide some form of benefit to us, or we can waste them away on the things that bring us sadness, misery, or simple negative emotions. Forgiveness allows us to put the energy that we have into something positive.

So where should it go? It should go to the places that can help us evolve in endeavors that bring us meaning. Meaning isn't found in misery. It's found in getting out of the hole one is in.

The greater purpose behind forgiveness is to find yourself. It's to find your own path toward life. The lessons that you've learned must be utilized to bring growth and progression in your life. Once you forgive and are able to move forward, you are at a stage where you understand the things that bring you joy and the things that don't.

Growth And Healing

Growth comes from pain. Growth does not come from being comfortable and happy. People grow the most after life hits them the hardest. As unfortunate as that sounds, it's a big part of the human experience. As we go through life, we encounter situations that make us uncomfortable.

We encounter events we never thought to be likely. In those moments of hardship, we learn a lot about ourselves, who we are as people, and what it actually means to be us. How we shape ourselves after we hit rock bottom is what defines us. When you hit rock bottom, you have nowhere to go but up.

The path to growth is to forgive, to let go, and to accept everything as is. This allows true emotional healing to begin, and you can finally become whole again.

Once you become whole, you can progress to the next stage of your future development. For everyone that's different, you might want to find love again, or you might want to devote your life to something you're passionate about, which could be anything really.

The freedom to do everything you've ever wanted is now here. You have the freedom to be whoever you want, with the added benefit of having a whole lot of experience. Many people look up to others who hold this wisdom and experience. Maybe you could do good for others in this time. You could help them grow as individuals just like you have done all this work to grow as a human being.

The memories will still haunt you from time to time; however, the pain will subside, it will be less intense, and the pain will be less frequent.

You will know when you have attained peace. The past will no longer hurt you. The memories will simply be something you look back fondly on and smile at.

Hopefully, by that point, you will have done the work needed because if so, you will have attained not only peace but also those desires, those dreams that bring you meaning.

Everything In Life Is Based On How You React

Read it again and internalize it. Situations in life, in a lot of cases, are beyond your control. There's not much you can do about them, but how you react is everything. How you react to a particular event or a situation is all that matters. What you do when things go badly is everything.

A painful tragedy is a test that life throws our way; we are never really prepared for it, but we have to face it with all our strength. Life is all about the unexpected, both the good and the bad. Much of the good that has happened to you, you might not have expected, just like the bad.

A person is an amalgamation of their experiences, both good and bad. All these experiences play a role in making us who we are.

Your reaction to a particular situation, whether good or bad, shapes your future.

So when you react in a productive way to a particular situation, you do the work that's needed to move on, and then you focus on doing the things that make you happy, this can bring you meaning and enable you to attain some form of fulfillment.

What Exactly Does Forgiveness Even Mean?

It can mean a lot of different things to a lot of different people. Forgiveness, however, is the idea that you let go of the feelings of resentment and anger that you might hold on to.

One can ask, "But why should I forgive?" It's because forgiveness opens the door to a positive future. No longer weighed down by the demons of the past, you are able to walk again, to move forward, to open your heart again.

The path forward is often not the easiest for everyone, but time and time again, throughout this book, I've mentioned how life isn't quite supposed to be easy. It's supposed to be a journey with challenges that grow you if you face them and allow them to grow you.

You Only Have Yourself So Forgive Yourself

The person you once loved and cherished is no longer with you, but you are still here, and more than anything, you're all you have left. Forgive yourself so you might be able to go through this journey because you don't know when the clock runs out on you, either.

More than anything, you have to forgive yourself for your health. Holding onto feelings of resentment or anger can cause your cortisol levels to rise to unprecedented levels.

No one should have to go through that because cortisol kills you in the long run. It's the stress hormone, and it's quite damaging to your body if it stays at elevated levels. If the level of cortisol within you stays elevated, the damage that it causes can make you die an early death and just, in general, worsen your quality of life.

Forgiveness allows you to focus on the thing that matters the most in your life: yourself. When you focus on yourself, you can move forward with just your life, and your life's journey becomes more about doing the things that enrich you and make you feel better about yourself.

Letting Go Of Negative Emotions

Negative emotions will drain you and hold you back from growing. That much is understood by everyone. But why do they hold us back? They hold us back because negative emotions are a form of weight on our souls. Negative emotions hold us back because, with every passing moment, we still keep thinking about the things that make us upset or make our lives miserable.

Understand Mindfulness

Mindfulness refers to a form of meditation that is all about becoming more aware of your thoughts, your feelings, and your bodily sensations within the present moment. The key to making it work properly is that you have no judgment. I'm going to be providing some tips that can help you learn and understand how mindfulness works:

1. Observe everything: Pay more attention to the things that are around you. This can be the food you eat, the air that you breathe, or the space you inhabit.

2. Mindful eating: Focus on the food you're eating and notice the little details, such as the taste, the texture, and the smell.

3. Scan your body: Feel out any pain you might be having, any tension, or something that you might find to be odd.

4. Meditate: This involves sitting in a quiet space, sitting straight up, closing your eyes, taking deep breaths, and noticing your breath as it enters and exits your mouth.

Make sure when you're meditating, you're sitting in a comfortable position.

Meditation Exercises

Quite a few ways exist to practice meditation. Let's take a look at some of the ways that meditation can be utilized so let's take a look at structured meditation exercises:

1. Body Scan Meditation: Lie on your back with your legs extended and your arms at your sides with your palms facing up. Focus all your attention deliberately on each part of your body.

2. Sitting meditation: Sit comfortably and with your back straight, your feet flat on the floor, and your hands in your lap. Breathe through your nose, focus on your breath, moving in and out of your body. If you feel physical sensations or thoughts that interrupt your meditation, pay attention to it and then return your focus to your breathing.

3. Walking meditation: Find a quiet place 10 to 20 feet in length, and begin to walk slowly. Pay attention to the experience of walking,

staying aware of the sensations of standing and also the subtle movements that will maintain your balance. Once you reach the end of your path, you turn and continue walking, all the while maintaining an awareness of the sensations.

The Idea Behind Mindfulness

The idea behind mindfulness is about being curious and non-judgmental, as well as having more awareness, paying close attention to the present moment, and having greater sensations and thoughts. The intention to cultivate your awareness must be there. Attention to the present moment is also a must.

You have to understand that for mindfulness to be effective, it takes a while. You need to have patience if you want it to work for you.

The Benefits Of Mindfulness And Meditation

There are many different benefits to meditation and mindfulness. The fact of the matter is that you benefit from it over time, which means you can't really expect it to cure all your problems in one day. So, how can you benefit from it?

1. Mindfulness Allows You To Understand Your Pain: This is quite important to understand. Pain is a fact of life. Mindfulness allows you to reshape and understand your relationship with pain.

2. A Better Connection: If you've ever been in a social setting and found it difficult to connect with someone or understand what they're saying, being more mindful allows you to give them far more attention and focus.

3. Reduced Stress: Mindfulness lowers the stress levels that exist within your body.

4. Increased focus: Meditation and mindfulness allow you to improve your innate ability to focus.

5. Reduces the noise: Oftentimes, we feel a lot of 'noise,' which refers to the voice in our head that often reminds us of the bad things in our lives. When we're trying to think or focus, the noise never seems to leave us alone and prevents us from focusing.

My Story Of Forgiveness

I held on to feelings of resentment. I'd ask, "Why Angela?" quite often. However, I did not feel as much guilt because I had done everything I possibly knew of. I did hold onto some feelings of resentment for leaving me alone in this world, but eventually, I forgave her for that and moved on from those feelings. Letting go brought me a greater sense of peace, and I was able to move forward much better.

Forgiveness Gives You The Space To Grow

The freedom to grow comes when you have forgiven yourself for all the mistakes of the past and have forgiven your lost love for leaving you too soon. It is only after you have forgiven yourself for the past that you can look forward to the future. Time waits for no one, and that's something we all have to remember.

Chapter 10: Embracing The Future– Final Reflections And Moving Forward With Purpose

The First Step Is The Hardest

You're alone, scared, upset and confused. You don't know what to do because something you never imagined happened to you. The only thing left now is to act in a way that's productive because if you choose to wallow in self-pity, eventually, you see the years pass by, with you becoming a shell of what you once were. Move forward with the mindset that you will find a way out of the situation you are in, but before you can move forward, you have to make a promise to yourself that you will do better for yourself because you are important. Every single thing that you feel is valid; however, once you feel the emotions, it's time to leave them behind and move past them.

Many tend to stay in one place and stagnate or decline when they encounter this sort of situation. It's never easy; it's the hardest thing that can happen to anyone, losing someone that they love the most in this world. However, you do not do the ones who've passed any favors by letting yourself get worse. That's not what they would have wanted for you. When you're with someone who loves you, they want you to do the best that you possibly can, and they don't want you to suffer miserably. So, honor their memory by moving forward with purpose.

So when you take the first step and move forward, you choose to make your life better for yourself rather than choosing to wallow in your self-pity and stay sad and depressed. You choose to make yourself happy again, no matter how rough the road is and no matter how difficult things get.

Defining your Purpose

What is purpose? How do we quantify or define it? Is it a subjective feeling or desire that exists among people? Or is it something else entirely? Purpose is something that is unique to every person out there. Someone's purpose is their true calling. The one thing they know is that when they do it, it gives them meaning. It could even be a dream they've always had. A person's purpose in life is not static; it's dynamic, and it evolves over time. Your purpose might be to make the people around you happy, or it could be a goal to create a business that does really well, benefits people, and solves a unique problem.

Sometimes, the time we spend alone allows us to find our purpose because when we're away from the noise, and we're more mindful of everything around us, we discover the voice that's inside of us and what it truly wants.

Finding your purpose is also a matter of trying different things that make you feel whole. Most people never really find it because finding your purpose means stepping out of your comfort zone and doing something you've never done before. Leaving your comfort zone is really not easy. It's called a comfort zone for a reason.

However, there is a pain associated with just staying in your comfort zone; that pain is the slow and gradual feeling that you're missing out on something you could have created for yourself.

A life that you've always wanted, slipping away day by day simply because you refuse to face the fears that have always held you back.

After a certain point, regardless of how tragic circumstances in your life might have turned out to be, you can't allow them to hold you back anymore because they can't be the events that define you forever. What defines you are your principles.

Make Sure You Mourn And Grieve

You have to learn to crawl before you can walk. The same principles apply here: you have to go through the grieving process. You have to let your emotions out and feel them thoroughly before you begin the journey to move forward. You need to express your emotions as much as you can because if you don't, they will hold you back. There will be a metaphorical weight on your shoulders that will eventually break you if you don't let it off.

Do the hard work before you can move forward with anything. No matter how long it takes, you have to go through it.

Get therapy as well. It's best to discuss your thoughts with someone who is professionally trained and equipped to deal with circumstances such as this.

Many of the problems that we face in life are caused simply by us refusing to let our emotions out.

Understand that letting go is the hardest thing to do in this world, but it is necessary. Regardless of how we feel about it, we have to move on, and we have to let go no matter what. We cannot allow the past to completely define our future.

You have to get out of the hole you're in, but you also have to fully feel the emotions you are going to be having.

You Have To Make A Move

If you lived in a particular place for a long period of time with someone, that place begins to hold symbolic value for you and your partner who is no longer with you. To truly move forward, you have to move to a different place, preferably in a different city or even country. A new place allows you to start your life again, so to speak because you cannot live life with the memories of the past, as they will constantly weigh you down and make you feel worse.

Write Your Thoughts Down: Productive Journaling Goes A Long Way

Writing your thoughts down helps you deal with a traumatic event. It allows you to look at things far more objectively, especially if you journal and speak to a therapist as well. It allows us to unpack many of the feelings that are pent up inside of us.

Find a schedule to journal every week or every day, find a comfortable spot, and write your thoughts down. Understand that it's something that will benefit you in the long run, and it won't provide a short-term solution. Just like everything else in life, consistency is key, and consistency will take you out of the hole you find yourself in.

Journaling helps greatly in observing the progress that you've made mentally. You just need to set the right expectations for yourself when you start journaling.

Having Strong Principles for A Good Future

A strong value system is to be utilized to craft meaningful values that you can use to live a just and righteous life that helps both you and the people around you. We don't exist on our own without people. We exist with the world, and the world exists with us. If we choose to be complacent and ignorant of the effect we have on the world, no matter how small, then we add to the negativity and pain collectively felt by people around the world. If we wish to see more good in this world, we have to set examples and lead by example. A value system can be anything; if you're religious, it could be your faith, or if you're less religious, I would suggest you look into philosophy, and thus your principles can be based on philosophical ideas. There are many ways to go about it, and everyone needs to find their own path when it comes to this.

The benefit of having values and principles is the fact that you understand the things that are for you and the things that are not. It allows you to live your life in a way that provides meaning.

Embrace A Healthy Lifestyle

Whether you see its benefits or not, a healthy body is conducive to a healthy mind. You can't expect to feel better about yourself if you simply ignore your health and allow your body to deteriorate. Embrace some form of fitness regimen involving the gym, sports, and a healthy eating lifestyle. It'll do your body good, you'll feel better, you'll have greater energy levels, and you'll be able to live longer. The benefits are endless.

If you can't commit yourself to the gym because you find it boring, I still suggest that you reconsider because doing things we don't particularly enjoy at the moment can eventually, over a period of time, become the very things we love doing. What I'm trying to say is the more difficult and uncomfortable something might be, the more likely it is to push you out of your comfort zone and propel you to grow as a person.

Obviously, I don't expect anyone to become a full-blown fitness freak. However, the benefits and results speak for themselves, and the endorphins released during exercise do an amazing job for anyone's mood.

I would alternatively also suggest you pick up a sport if the gym is something you absolutely cannot do because you don't want to. A sport also allows you to engage with others, thus increasing your social circle and allowing you to form stronger connections with people.

Stimulate Your Mind Intellectually

Learn something new, a new language or a skill perhaps, something that requires you to think outside of the box. Grow your mind because learning never stops. No matter how old you get, you have a lot to learn. No one can truly ever learn everything. The world we live in is one where learning something new is a lot easier than it once was. It's simply due to the fact that the ease of access we have now to solid information is ridiculous.

Resources on the internet exist in abundance, and you can learn anything you'd ever want through courses alone, some free, some paid. Either way, you gain something useful because knowledge is a powerful thing.

The purpose of learning is more than just improving potential career prospects. Learning allows you to enhance your mind, and it can even help prevent mental decline as you age. As well as increasing your problem solving abilities.

Enrolling in college for another degree that you're interested in is another way to expand your mind and learn more.

Reinvent Yourself

Do whatever needs to be done to find yourself again because sharing so much time with one person tends to make it difficult for us to remember who we used to be. Start doing the things that make you happy again, step out of your comfort zone, and learn more about the world so you can grow as a person again.

Never stop trying in your pursuit of happiness, as you have a lot to learn and relearn because we forget so much about who we were when we encounter a situation where we lose someone with whom we spent a significant amount of time. A long-term relationship can often lead to people's lives being defined by the relationship, which means when it ends, they feel as if they've lost themselves. Life is all about growth and learning new things, so do as much as you can to find out who you truly are.

Do things that make you feel happy, and find something that fascinates you and gives you a sense of purpose. Once we find our new purpose, we end up becoming whole again, and that's truly a beautiful thing.

Suppose you want to help the poor and start a charity or maybe start an animal shelter because you care for little animals. I'm just brainstorming, but these are just a couple of things that can help you find your purpose. At the end of the day, you have to find out for yourself what you want from this world.

Express Yourself Through Creativity

Do something creative, whether it's art, music, or writing. Express your emotions through whatever art form you choose. It's not only therapeutic, but it's also an empowering feeling when you create something and share it with the world because it might resonate with someone who shares what you're going through. Our innate ability to be creative is a powerful gift that we are bestowed with, so utilize it and do something with it.

I utilized writing and wrote three books to share the struggles I was going through. That helped me tremendously because I was able to translate what I was feeling into something that could help others; it not only brought me a sense of accomplishment but also lifted a weight off my shoulders.

So, the long and short of it is creative self-expression is a powerful thing that we need to make more use of.

Make Friends, As Many As You Can

Socialize as much as you can, find new people, and keep looking for more avenues to socialize because we are meant to be with others, and we are meant to spend time with people because we are social creatures. If we stay alone and don't try to expand our social circles, we eventually find ourselves miserable and unhappy with our lot in life because no matter how much money we have or how many achievements we've made in our lives, without meaningful connections, it doesn't bring us the same level of happiness. We have to build connections no matter what. Every moment of joy we have is with other people and not alone. Every personal victory becomes sweeter when celebrating it with the ones we love and care about.

Another great benefit of having friends is the fact that they fill many of the gaps left behind by the partner you once had. Friends help you feel like you're not truly lonely because you have someone to share something with. We have emotional and social needs that we just can't give up on; they are needs for a reason, and they need to be met.

Don't Give Up On Love

You're still alive and breathing, and you still have a heart. Share it with someone. You might find it difficult but do it anyway because you only have one life to live, and you have to spend it doing the things that matter to you. Loving someone is the greatest joy that life can possibly give us. We should not live life with the fear that we might get hurt again because fear should not dictate our actions or decisions. Life is all about making new experiences and finding your own path to happiness, so try doing that. The benefit of socializing and making new friends, along with doing hobbies that involve other people, is that you are better equipped to find and make new friends and possible romantic connections that will help you find happiness again.

To experience true love again, you have to understand that a connection is built between two people. That you are half of the connection. The relationship you had with your partner, who was with you, was so special because of you, just as much as it was because of them. You were the other half that made that connection so special; don't forget that when you try to build a connection with someone again. You are just as important as they were.

Obviously, by the time you find love again, you will have done the hard work needed to move forward and grow as a person. You would have gone through the seven stages of grief and evolved as a person. You would have mourned the loss of someone so important to you and grown as a result of it.

It's important that before you find love again, you go through every single aspect of the grieving process and rediscover who you are as a person. Otherwise, your emotions will be all over the place when you do try to start a relationship with someone else. It's not fair to your new partner, and it's not fair to you either when you haven't put the past behind you.

One thing to keep in mind is that for any new love to flourish, you and your new partner have to be on the same page. You have to make sure that your values align and that they want the same things as you do. So go out there, make connections, and find love, but understand that what makes a relationship strong and long-lasting is when people communicate effectively to one another about what they want and what they don't.

How I Have Managed To Progress So Far

I am currently in very good health. I have six-month appointments with my health provider, and this also includes extensive lab work. My health provider is very pleased with my health so far. I have also made many new friends and, along with them, many great memories, which has helped a great deal because socialization has helped me a lot.

The happiest achievement since Angela's passing has been the new friends that I have made. As I mentioned earlier in the book, socialization is quite important for every human being.

I also had some travel plans. I planned to travel to Israel; however, the war forced me to stay back home, so now I'm planning a trip to Hawaii, which was Angela's and my favorite winter destination.

It's A Beautiful World Out There, So Enjoy It

The world is such a beautiful place with plenty of opportunities for anyone who is willing to take them. When we move forward with purpose, we discover so much of the beauty that exists within the world. Our lives are a gift, and we should allow ourselves to enjoy them while we still can.

About the Author

Patrick Palmer's caregiving journey began in 2011 when his wife, Angela, was diagnosed with Stage IV brain cancer. Over the next fifty-three months, Patrick devoted himself to Angela's care, providing her with love, strength, and unwavering dedication as she faced the challenges of glioblastoma multiforme. After Angela's passing in 2016 at the age of 68, Patrick turned to writing as a way to process his grief and honor her memory.

What began as a personal journaling exercise evolved into a mission to support others in similar circumstances. *Patrick* wrote three books, and "Time to Move Forward" is the last step of his caregiving journey. These books draw deeply from his own experiences, offering heartfelt insights and practical advice for those caring for loved ones during life's most difficult moments.

Today, *Patrick* is a passionate advocate for caregivers and cancer research. His work continues to inspire and uplift readers, providing them with the tools and encouragement needed to face caregiving challenges with resilience and compassion. *Patrick*'s dedication to this cause is both a tribute to Angela and a testament to his commitment to fostering a stronger, more supported caregiving community.

Made in the USA
Columbia, SC
17 February 2025